Monkeys

A captivating look at these fascinating animals

Introduction

MONKEYS, APES, lemurs, and their cousins are collectively called primates. These close cousins of ourselves are many things: active and curious, sociable and communicative, and often disconcertingly intelligent. They are widely varied creatures, yet they show many similar features. Some are almost too common and abundant in number and become irritating food-stealing pests, while others are perilously rare in their fast-disappearing habitats.

The lemur group includes well-known species such as the ring-tailed lemur and ruffed lemur, as well as the scarce, mysteriously nocturnal aye-aye. Closely related are the huge-eyed galagos or bushbabies, lorises, and pottos. Monkeys range from tiny tamarins and marmosets to large, powerful baboons with long, fierce-looking canine teeth. The apes are the monkeys' bigger, tail-less relatives. They include the lesser apes, or gibbons, and the greater apes — orang-utans, gorillas, and chimpanzees.

From the lemurs, through the monkeys to the great apes, there is an overall trend toward more complex behavior, including increasing intelligence, strong family ties and sophisticated displays of feelings and emotions. This trend continues through to human beings, since we are the great apes' closest living relatives. We recognize many traits in them that we know in ourselves. The study of lemurs, monkeys, and apes not only helps us to understand, appreciate, and conserve these fascinating creatures. It also provides an excellent background to understanding the human condition, and leads to greater appreciation of our own origins, and perhaps where we may be heading.

Above: Unlike many primates, ring-tailed lemurs spend a large proportion of their time on the ground.

Opposite: The orang-utan or 'red ape' is the most arboreal, or tree-dwelling, member of the great ape family.

FAMILIES AND COUSINS

Monkeys, apes, lemurs, and their relatives comprise more than a dozen of the groupings known as families. These families are linked by shared features, such as the structure of the face, shoulder, and hand. But there is also great variation between them. In the great ape family, a mature male gorilla can weigh more than 441lb (200kg) — as much as three adult humans. At the other end of the spectrum, in the dwarf lemur family, the pygmy mouse lemur weighs 6000 times less, at just 1oz (30g), and is as diminutive as a mouse.

Uniting Features

MONKEYS, APES, and other primates have their place in the wondrous scheme we call the natural world. But where do they fit in? How do they relate to other animals in terms of their evolutionary history, and how did they come to be as they are?

Scientists classify the living world into a hierarchy of groups. Animals with backbones are known as vertebrates, and vertebrates with warm blood, fur or hair and mammary (milk-making) glands to feed their young, are known as mammals. Among the mammals are the three broad groupings of the monkeys, the apes, and the lemurs and their cousins. These three share certain features that unite them into a larger category — the order Primates (pronounced 'pry-mate-eez'). Its members are called primates ('pry-mates').

Primates and other mammals

Primates have the general features possessed by all mammals. If we look in more detail, however, it becomes clear that primates share particular features with four other kinds of mammals:

- Insectivores (350 species) such as shrews, moles, hedgehogs, moonrats, and tenrecs.
- Bats (about 1000 species), the only mammals capable of sustained powered flight.
- Tree-shrews or tupaids (only 20 or so species), which resemble a combination of shrew and squirrel, and live in South and Southeast Asia.
- Colugos (just two species), restricted to Southeast Asia. Often called 'flying lemurs' from their facial appearance, they are not true lemurs, and not true fliers but expert gliders.

There are several areas where the similarity between primates and these four groups can be identified. Some scientific similarities are related to body anatomy, especially the form of the upper limb and shoulder bones, and the arrangement of wrist and hand bones. Others concern the size of the brain relative to the body, and the shape of the brain's parts or lobes. Natural body substances, such as disease-fighting antibody chemicals, also correspond well between these mammals and primates. So does their genetic material, as determined by tests similar to those popularly called DNA fingerprinting.

Overall, probably the primates' closest living cousins are the colugos and tree-shrews. The latter, especially, are regarded as 'primitive' mammals. This means they resemble the very first mammals to appear on Earth, at the beginning of the Age of Dinosaurs more than 200 million years ago.

Primate features

Primates are often viewed as fairly 'typical' mammals, which means they retain many of the original mammalian features. They have departed much less from the ancestral mammal body plan compared to, for example, elephants with their extraordinary long trunks, or horses with their single-toed feet, or

dolphins with their flipper-like front limbs. But several features mark out the primates from other mammals. They include:

- A relatively large brain compared to the size (in terms of weight or volume) of the body.
- Forward-facing eyes (rather than eyes on the side of the head, as in rabbits and mice). These have good vision and color perception, and are able to judge distance accurately, as explained later.
- An ability to jump and leap with great agility, partly due to the structure of the mobile, flexible shoulder and hip joints.
- Dexterous hands and feet, with digits — fingers and toes — able to grasp and manipulate (rather than the paws or hoofed feet of other mammals).
- Flattened nails on the digits in most primate species, rather than sharp claws or blunt hooves.

In terms of lifestyle and habitat, most lemurs, monkeys, and apes live in sociable groups, have complicated interactions with their group members, provide a relatively long period of parental care for their young and depend on trees for their habitat and food supply. The majority of primate species live in tropical forests and use trees for shelter, homes, movement, food, and overall survival. Only a few are more at home on the ground, such as the baboons — and human beings. Members of the human species have all the typical primate features, and we are members of the primate group.

Previous pages: The forward-facing eyes of primates such as this gorilla (left) allow excellent depth perception, also called binocular vision. Mutual grooming, observed here in Japanese macaques (right), is an important social interaction in many primates.

Left: Gibbons like the lar gibbon excel at the primates' ability to use their mobile limbs skillfully as they hold on, swing, walk, and leap through the branches of trees.

Opposite: Among all animals, primates have the most manipulative hands, ideal for holding branches and picking food items.

Monkeys

ALERT AND active, noisy and chattering, a monkey troop travels through the tropical forest branches, on the lookout for food and danger. Most monkeys use a variety of methods for movement, including leaps, arm-swings from branch to branch, and running on all fours along bigger boughs. As the midday sun beats down, the troop settles to rest. Some doze, while others groom themselves or their 'special companions' as part of the many and complicated social interactions within the group. By late afternoon the stifling heat fades, and the troop is on the go again. They grab soft leaves and juicy fruits to eat, wastefully throw away much of their pickings after just a bite or two, and all the while watch their neighbors. If one of the troop locates an especially rich source of tasty buds or blossom, the others crowd around and a bout of bickering breaks out.

This description could apply to the great majority of monkeys. The exact number of monkey species is difficult to estimate, since new ones are still being discovered. Another complicating factor occurs when what was thought to be a single monkey species is shown by genetic and other studies to be several very similar species, as described below.

General monkey features include five-fingered hands and five-toed feet that can grasp and hold; also legs that are longer than the arms (considerably longer in species that jump and leap often), and a tail as long as, or lengthier than, the head and body. However this last attribute, the tail, has been almost lost in a few species.

Monkeys fall into two major groups. These are commonly known as the New World monkeys, occupying the 'New World' of the Americas, chiefly Central and South America, and the Old World monkeys, which live on the 'Old World' continents including Africa and Asia.

New World monkeys

There are more than 140 species of New World monkeys. Their exact classification is a subject of some dispute but a general list of the main groups includes:

- Marmosets and tamarins.
- Capuchins and squirrel monkeys.
- Titi monkeys.
- Night or owl monkeys, also called douroucoulis.
- Sakis and uakaris.
- Howler monkeys.
- Spider and woolly monkeys.

Compared to the Old World species, American monkeys tend to be smaller and more arboreal, or tree-dwelling, so they are less likely to be seen on the ground. Most kinds favor dense tropical forests, especially the rainforests of the vast Amazon region in north-central South America. There are also species in the smaller rainforest areas of Central America.

The largest New World monkeys are the howlers, with the mantled howler and black howler weighing more than 22lb (10kg). They have proportionally large faces and a voicebox specialized to produce their astonishingly penetrating whoops and howls. These calls are mainly to proclaim territory and are the loudest sounds produced by any land animal. Howler monkeys spend more time on the ground than the smaller species, perhaps over one-quarter of their day, as they move between feeding areas and also stop occasionally to groom each other.

The marmosets and tamarins are generally the smallest of the New World monkeys. They are active and darting, with long fur and small faces. Several species have contrasting fur colors on the upper lip, leading to names such as the emperor tamarin, which sports a luxuriant white mustache set against generally black head hair.

Previous pages: Most smaller monkeys (left) have little, rounded, large-eyed, snub-nosed faces, and ears partly hidden in the fur. Vervet monkeys (right) range widely across Africa's varied habitats.

Opposite: The black howler usually has only one baby at a time.

Above right: Common squirrel monkeys often follow, or mix with, troops of capuchin monkeys.

Noses

The New World monkeys are also known as Neotropical primates, and by the scientific term Platyrrhini, 'flat noses'. This refers to one of the main ways of distinguishing them from the Old World monkeys. The New World monkey's nose is relatively broad or wide and flattened, and the nostrils tend to be angled so they face partly sideways, rather than opening to the front or downward. Also New World monkeys have more molar (cheek or chewing) teeth, 12 in total, compared to the eight molar teeth of Old World monkeys.

The prehensile tail

Not all monkeys have tails that are prehensile, or capable of gripping. But if one does, then it must be a New World species, since no Old World monkeys have this useful feature. It is most developed among the spider monkeys, which are among the most tree-dwelling of all primates. Just the last one-fifth of a spider monkey's tail can wrap around a bough and still support the animal's entire weight. The skin on the underside of the tail tip is hairless and bears ridges and grooves equivalent to our own fingerprints. This gives great sensitivity to touch and also provides a firm grip on damp, slippery bark.

The prehensile tail has many uses. In conjunction with the limbs, it helps to spread the animal's weight between several thin branches for greater security. Along with the two legs, it can grip to provide a secure tripod-like anchor that leaves both hands free to manipulate food. It is also able to pass food and other items to the mouth if the hands are occupied.

New World diets

New World monkeys are principally vegetarian. Most kinds eat a wide range of buds, blossoms, fruits, seeds, and other plant matter. Several species specialize in sap, gum, and other exudates. These are liquids that ooze from trees when the bark is stripped, usually with the teeth.

Many capuchins and titis consume some animal prey, ranging from caterpillars, grubs, and beetles to small lizards and baby birds, although most of their diet consists of plant matter. The common squirrel monkey has taken meat-eating to a greater degree and crunches up snails and crabs as well as spiders and a variety of other creepy-crawlies.

Top: Some types of squirrel monkey enjoy a wide diet, ranging from insects to sweet flower nectar.

Above: Many marmosets are gum and sap specialists, but will also eat buds and fruits.

Opposite: More than half the diet of the white-faced saki (this is a female, the male has an almost all-white face) consists of fruit. However, they have been known to catch live prey including bats.

Social behavior

New World monkeys show a wide range of social behavior. Spider monkeys dwell in large bands that divide into smaller groups as they forage for food, then meet up again at the end of the day. Squirrel monkeys form rambling troops, which regularly mix with other monkey species. Smaller subgroups often come and go, and the males and females do not form strong pair bonds. By contrast, in most marmosets the social unit is a breeding adult pair, their young and part-grown sub-adults who help with 'childcare.'

Old World monkeys

There are more than 130 species, or distinct types, of Old World monkeys in Africa and Asia. There are several ways of classifying them but these are the main groups that are generally recognized:

- Swamp monkeys, talapoins, patas, vervets, monas, and guenons.
- Macaques, mangabeys, baboons, drills, and mandrills.
- Colobus monkeys, guerezas, langurs, lutungs, leaf monkeys, douc monkeys, surilis, and snub-nosed monkeys.
- Tarsiers are sometimes included as Old World monkeys, or more often, as close cousins of them (see page 51).

The scientific name of the Old World monkey group is Catarrhini, 'narrow nose.' In contrast to New World monkeys, the nose is narrow or at least less broad, and the nostrils face forward or downward. Most Old World monkeys have eight molar or chewing teeth, not 12 as in New World types. No Old World monkey has a prehensile or grasping tail, and some kinds have virtually no tail at all, such as certain baboons.

Old World monkeys are generally heavy in build, with relatively large faces and stocky bodies. They tend to be more at home on the ground, again especially the baboons. Some species are extremely fast runners on all fours, like the patas monkey, which can bound along faster than a human can run.

Above: In northwest South America, capuchin monkeys forage mainly in the middle layers of the forest. They associate with uakaris, squirrel monkeys and several other monkey species.

Opposite: The characteristic features of Old World monkeys are well illustrated by this Japanese macaque — a narrow nose, downward-facing nostrils and a taller, slimmer, more angular face than New World species.

Fur coats

Fur length and coloration varies greatly among Old World monkeys. Many macaques are drab brown or gray. However other species have more impressive features. The lion-tailed macaque's pale, lion-like mane contrasts with its black-furred body and limbs. The male mandrill, the largest monkey at more than 55lb (25kg) — well over twice the weight of any New World species — has a startling red and blue-and-white-striped snout set off by an orange beard. The black-and-white colobus group are well named for their vividly contrasting coloration. The guenons are known for their facial coloration, which exhibits variations on a theme. The mustached guenon has a small, neat, white mustache, while in the white-throated guenon the white fur forms a beard and side 'whiskers' up to the ears.

Several kinds of Old World monkey have sitting pads, also known scientifically as ischial callosities. These are thickened patches or calluses of skin on the buttocks and rump. The appearance of these patches indicates the sex and maturity of the owner. In some species the patches become very colorful at breeding time.

Above: There are several kinds of black-and-white colobus found in different regions of Africa. The amount of white in the tails of these handsome monkeys varies between species from less than 10 percent to 90 percent.

Left: Each species and even subspecies of guenon features a slightly different pattern and color of facial hair. Lowe's guenon from coastal West Africa, pictured here, is one of several subspecies of Campbell's guenon.

Opposite: The male mandrill's colorful face brightens slightly in the breeding season to signal his readiness to mate. This large monkey is found in Cameroon and Gabon, West Africa.

Old World diets

The Old World monkeys are generally less reliant than their New World cousins on undisturbed tropical rainforest habitats to provide their dietary needs. Many forage on the ground for food and have omnivorous, opportunistic tastes. They pick seeds, buds, and shoots at ground level, and some dig for succulent tubers and other underground plant parts. They also grab small creatures like worms and insects, and catch larger prey including frogs, lizards, mice, and other rodents.

There are some specialized eaters among Old World monkeys. The crab-eating macaque really does eat crabs, although usually as an occasional dietary item, as well as frogs, young turtles, baby waterbirds, and other aquatic animals. However the colobines, which include the African colobus species and the Asian langurs and leaf monkeys, take little or no animal items. They have a specialized stomach with pouches. Here their main food of leaves is broken down and digested with the help of bacteria, much as cows 'ferment' their grassy food in a multi-chambered stomach.

Troops and families

With regard to social groups and interactions, Old World monkeys are generally more limited than their New World counterparts. Some Old World species, including macaques and baboons, form mixed troops of males, females, and young. The males may fight viciously to gain a higher position in the social rank or 'pecking order.'

In other Old World species, like guenons and langurs, the usual social unit is one male and his 'harem' of several females with their young. As the juvenile females grow, they may transfer allegiance to another group. However the young males roam alone or form bachelor troops, before they become mature and powerful enough to attract females and establish their own harems.

Top: The crab-eating, or long-tailed, macaque occurs widely through Southeast Asia but, despite its name, it eats mainly fruits and seeds.

Above: Individual members of a baboon troop soon get to know the new youngsters in their group as they identify them by sight, scent, and sound.

Opposite: Ebony langurs (this is a rare brown variant) care for their babies for about 18 months, after which they can fend for themselves.

Apes

THE APE group of primates has fewest members and is entirely Old World — apart from one species. There are two main subgroups:
- Lesser apes (family Hylobatidae). These are the gibbons or hylobatids, with about a dozen species (exact estimates range from 11 to 13), all in Southern and Southeast Asia.
- Great or greater apes (family Hominidae). These include the two species of orang-utan in Southeast Asia, and two species of gorilla plus two species of chimpanzee, all in Africa.

All humans, including the various extinct prehistoric types and the single living species *Homo sapiens* — ourselves — are also placed in the great ape family. We are the only species not limited to Africa or Southeast Asia.

Humans apart, in some ways the apes are larger versions of monkeys. But the ape group also has its distinctive physical features. One is the tail, or rather, lack of it. Most monkeys and other primates have tails, but no ape is tailed. However the use of the term

'ape' can be misleading. The so-called Barbary ape is tail-less, but then it is not a true ape. It is a type of monkey, a macaque, from the Atlas Mountains of Northwest Africa.

Gibbons

The gibbons form a closely similar group of smaller apes, occupying various geographic regions from East India, through the Southeast Asian mainland and the Malay Peninsula, into the islands of Sumatra, Java, and Borneo. The dozen or so kinds of gibbon probably evolved from a single ancestral species within the past two million years. During this time the map of South and Southeast Asia was different to today's map. It changed many times as sea levels rose and fell, isolating different parts of the region as islands. The ancestral gibbons were separated on these islands and so evolved to become different species, each suited to its own particular habitat.

Gibbons have smallish faces, lightweight bodies, long legs, and very long, muscular arms with hook-like

hands. The long, arched fingers are set close together, and the thumb is very reduced (small). This hand structure is linked to gibbons' method of arm-swinging through the branches, known as brachiation. It consists of a series of pendulum-like swings, using the hands as hooks over the branches while maintaining forward body momentum. Gibbons can travel more than five times faster through the forest canopy than any animal could run down below at ground level.

The largest gibbon, known as the siamang, has a head-body length of up to 35in (90cm) and may weigh in excess of 33lb (15kg). (This is less than half the weight of the smallest great ape, the bonobo or pygmy chimpanzee.) The female siamang, as in most ape species, is smaller than the male. This difference between the sexes is known scientifically as sexual dimorphism, although it is less marked among the gibbons than it is in the great apes. The smallest species include Kloss's gibbon and the white-handed gibbon, which may be only half the siamang's size.

Gibbon habitat

In general, gibbons live among the branches of primary or undisturbed tropical forests, eat fruits and leaves, and live in small family groups led by a female and male who form a strong, long-lasting pair bond. They reinforce this bond regularly, especially during the 'dawn chorus,' by their calls. These consist of various noises, such as whoops, hollers, screeching, and what seems like cackling human laughter. The male and female gibbon 'duet,' calling out and answering each other. The sounds announce that the pair are healthy and in occupation of their territory, or patch of forest, so that others of their kind should stay away.

Most gibbons are principally fruit-eaters. In these species fruits make up more than half of the diet. Siamangs eat mostly leaves, while up to a quarter of the food of Kloss's gibbon includes small animal items, such as caterpillars, termites, beetles, and grubs.

Previous pages: Young chimps (left) test-taste all kinds of food. Most gibbons (right) live in small groups comprising a female, male, and offspring from the past few years.

Above: Gibbons are able to run upright along branches, using their long arms to grasp nearby boughs or held out for balance.

Opposite: Gibbons like this white-handed, or lar, gibbon rarely come down to the ground, and then usually only to consume small quantities of mineral-rich soil or to forage for insects.

Orang-utans

The only Asian great apes are the orang-utans, with two species, the Bornean orang-utan *Pongo pygmaeus* and the Sumatran orang-utan *Pongo abelii*. Until the 1990s the two species were regarded as one, with the Sumatran orang-utan classed as a subspecies of the Bornean orang. But genetic studies have confirmed their separate status, indicating that the two species have been evolving independently for more than a million years.

Orang-utans have distinctive reddish hair or fur, although the exact shade varies between individuals, from dark rusty-brown or maroon to bright orange. The hair tends to be coarser and shorter in the Bornean species. Mature and older males develop enlarged cheek pads (pouches or flanges), which greatly widen the face, and which are covered with fine pale hair in the Sumatran species. Bornean males also have a long chin pouch. In both species, older males also grow a cloak-like fringe of longer hairs hanging from the shoulders and arms.

Orang-utans are the most tree-dwelling of the great apes. Older males may move on the ground, walking upright with arms held aloft, but females and juveniles rarely descend from the branches. Orang-utans are also the most solitary of the great apes, contrasting greatly with the gorillas and chimps. They may congregate at rich food sources such as fruiting durian trees, but generally they travel and sleep alone, apart from a mother with her young.

The orang-utan's typical diet is based on plants, especially ripe fruits, along with leaves, blossom, and shoots. However, they also take animal matter, from termites, small grubs and honey to bird eggs and chicks, and even tree rats and young squirrels.

Above and opposite: The name orang-utan means 'old man of the forest' in the local Malay language. Older males (right) are distinguished by their fleshy cheek flanges, a sign of maturity that also includes throat pouches, which are absent from both adult females and from unflanged males. Females (above) have slightly shorter fur than males but also sport a beard-like growth of facial hair.

Gorillas

The largest of the apes, and biggest primates, are the gorillas. A big male may stand more than 5.9ft (1.8m) tall and weigh 441lb (200kg), although the average is nearer 353-375lb (160-170kg). Gorillas also reveal the biggest size difference between the sexes, with males often being twice the size of females. In appearance, most gorillas are well muscled with black hair, except on the black facial skin. Older males develop a light or gray tinge on the back and flanks and are known as silverbacks.

Some experts have listed as many as five species. Modern views now limit this to two. One is the Western gorilla, *Gorilla gorilla*. This is found in West Africa, in scattered regions forming an arc from Nigeria and Cameroon to the Central African Republic, Democratic Republic of Congo, and Angola. Generally two subspecies are recognized — the Western lowland gorilla and Cross River gorilla.

The Eastern gorilla, *Gorilla beringei*, is found more than 620 miles (1000km) away from its western counterpart, in Central Africa. It includes the Eastern lowland gorilla from eastern DR Congo across to southwestern Uganda and south to northern Rwanda. The other kinds of Eastern gorillas are the mountain gorillas. These have much longer hair than other gorillas, as an adaptation to their chilly, wet, high-altitude homelands. They are critically threatened and found only in small areas straddling the borders of DR Congo, Uganda, and Rwanda.

Gorillas are primarily forest vegetarians. They alter their diet through the seasons, consuming flowers, leaves, and fruits, supplemented by less nutritious items such as bark and herbs. Western gorillas are more likely to eat animal items, especially termites and ants, also caterpillars and grubs. Eastern gorillas focus even more on plant foods, including shoots and buds, vines, stems, and roots in their diet.

The standard gorilla social unit comprises one mature dominant male, the silverback, with three to five females and their offspring. As the youngsters grow, they usually leave their birth group and team up to form new groups that try to establish their own territories. Compared to chimpanzees, it is rare for a gorilla family group to split into two or more, or for several groups to merge.

Below: The difference in fur length between the different gorilla types is well demonstrated by this young mountain gorilla (below left) and the lowland gorilla youngster with its mother (below).

Opposite: Gray hairs are just starting to appear on this maturing male gorilla. He will not become a silverback until about 12 years of age, when a distinctive patch of gray hair will start to cover his back.

Chimpanzees

The two species of chimpanzee are the well-known and familiar chimpanzee or chimp, also called the common or robust chimpanzee, *Pan troglodytes*, and the bonobo, occasionally known as the pygmy chimpanzee, *Pan paniscus*. Chimps live in West and Central Africa, from Senegal through Nigeria to Congo, Angola, and Zambia. Bonobos are found only in a small region of DR Congo, south of the River Congo and its tributary the Lualaba.

The common chimp male is typically 31in (80cm) in head-body length, stands around 43in (110cm) tall, and weighs 99-121lb (45-55kg). The female is around 22lb (10kg) lighter. Hair color is black, with gray on the back in older individuals. Youngsters have pink or light brown facial skin that darkens with age, so a pink-faced chimp is a young individual.

The bonobo, despite its name of 'pygmy' chimp, is about as tall as the chimpanzee, but more slender and lightly built — what zoologists call gracile. Typically a bonobo is around 11-22lb (5-10kg) lighter than a chimpanzee of the same height. The bonobo also has proportionately longer limbs, a narrower chest, dark or black face skin from an early age, and a center parting of head hair.

Above: Bonobos often feed on the ground, mainly on herbaceous vegetation, but also on insects and small animals. Their groups tend to be smaller than those of common chimpanzees, and are usually dominated by females rather than males.

Right: Chimpanzee youngsters are weaned by about four years old, but stay near their mothers for another year or two. They reach puberty between the ages of eight and ten, and can live to around 40 years of age in the wild.

Opposite: Chimps have relatively large ears, and these and the face are hairless. Each individual chimpanzee has a unique pattern of facial skin coloring.

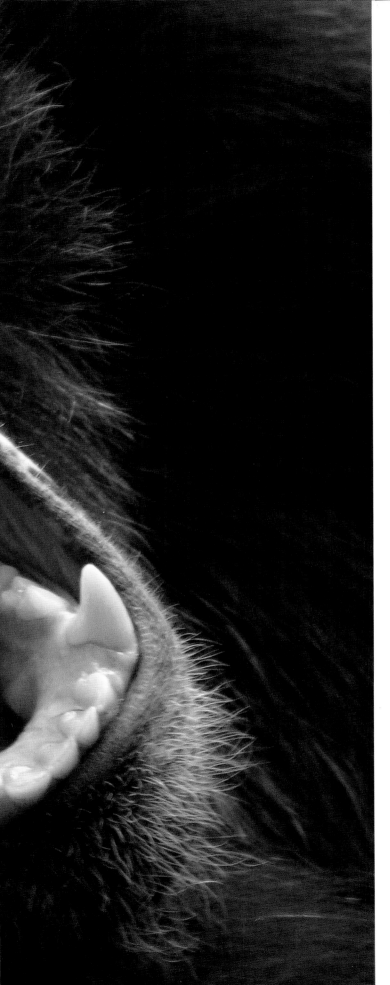

Chimp food and society

Chimps occupy a wide range of habitats, from dense tropical forest to scattered bush-savannah. More than all other apes (apart from us) and even primates, chimps have a very wide-ranging diet. Their food sources vary hugely with the seasons, from shoots and fruits to termites, honey, plant bulbs, and bark. Common chimps are known for their raucous hunting expeditions, where they cooperate to kill other creatures. Victims range from small monkeys to wild pigs and bushbucks, and even a chimp from a neighboring troop that has strayed into their territory, as is described later in the book.

Common chimpanzee society is likewise complicated and diverse. Generally a group of related males is dominant and defends the territorial boundaries; it is these individuals that form hunting parties. Females and their offspring come and go, and band together in twos and threes for a time before moving on.

Bonobos tend to have a more laid-back approach compared to common chimps. Their social groups change less often, and there is less outright hostility between neighboring troops. They eat animal foods but do not form large hunting parties. Bonobos are also known for their frequent display of sexual acts, either simulated or actual, and between individuals of all ages, adults and young. Their purpose is usually to strengthen friendship bonds and establish which individuals are dominant and submissive, as shown on later pages.

Left: An adult chimpanzee is a formidable adversary and bares its teeth to show threat or anger. On either side of the small front incisor teeth, the four canines are long and sharp. They can inflict serious wounds on rivals as well as tear apart the victims of gang hunts. The cheek teeth or molars are used to crush leaves, fruits, seeds, and other tough plant foods.

Relationships: them and us

It was once believed that the African great apes — chimps and gorillas — formed one closely related group, while humans occupied another, more separate group. It is now clear that humans and chimps are most closely related. The genetic material, DNA, of chimpanzees was formerly thought to be 98-99 percent similar to our own. This figure has recently been amended to nearer 95 percent, although the differences are mostly in what is sometimes known as 'junk' DNA, the exact function of which is unclear. However, this DNA analysis does show that of all animals, chimps are our closest living relatives.

Evidence suggests that the evolutionary paths of chimpanzees and bonobos diverged between two and three million years ago. Humans split from the chimp-bonobo branch some six to seven million years ago. Before this, gorillas had separated from the chimp-human line around seven to nine million years ago.

Going back farther, the 'original great ape' existed around 14-15 million years ago, when its kind split into the orang-utan branch for Asia and the gorilla-chimp-human branch in Africa. Even before this, the 'original ape' existed about 17-19 million years ago, when its evolutionary branches divided into the lesser apes or gibbons, and to the great ape lineages of orang, gorilla, chimp, and human.

Above: Gorillas are the next closest living relatives to humans after the two chimpanzee species and are considered to be highly intelligent in respect of interactions with their environment.

Left: Gorillas and chimpanzees display many similarities to humans, especially in aspects of their behavior such as family life, social relationships, and the extended care and protection of their offspring.

Opposite: Thoughtful, intentional, emotional — great apes like the chimpanzee share many of our mental faculties, as well as the vast majority of our genetic material. Human and chimp genome analyses may help in understanding some human diseases.

Lemurs and Cousins

THE MONKEYS and apes form one major grouping within the primates, the haplorrhines or 'dry noses.' The other main group is the strepsirrhines or 'wet noses.' They are divided into about seven families — four of lemurs, along with the lorises, the pottos, and the galagos or bushbabies. In evolutionary history the wet- and dry-noses probably separated more than 60 million years ago, at a time when the dinosaurs had only just become extinct.

Lemurs

Lemurs live in the wild only on the large island of Madagascar, off the southeast coast of Africa, plus associated small islands in the region. In the unique fauna of Madagascar, lemurs fill the roles of monkeys, bushbabies, and other primates, which are absent on the island. The different species occupy varied habitats, from thick forest to open bush.

In body form the typical lemur has a more protruding muzzle than a monkey or ape, along with limbs of roughly equal length, or legs longer than

arms, and a long, balancing but non-prehensile tail. A lemur also tends to hold its body more horizontal than apes and monkeys, and has grasping hands and feet for a life in the branches, with the characteristic primate feature of nails rather than claws on the fingers and toes. For these and other reasons, lemurs are regarded as more primitive — that is, more similar to the original primate ancestor — than monkeys and apes. This explains the derivation of the older term 'prosimian,' meaning 'before ape/monkey.'

Most lemurs have a base color for their fur of brown, gray, or reddish. However, some feature distinctive contrasting patterns, especially on the head and tail, like the black-and-white face and tail bands of the ring-tailed lemur. Strangely, some lemur species reveal very different coloration between their subspecies or varieties. For example, the ruffed lemur is named for the long fur on its ears and the sides of its head. The black-and-white variety of ruffed lemur is indeed black and white, with different markings in each individual. However, the red variety of ruffed

lemur is mostly rusty or light chestnut-brown, with black only on the crown of the head, and white only on the back of the neck. Such color variations make it difficult to identify some lemur species.

Ghosts and specters

The name 'lemur' is derived from an ancient Latin term meaning 'night spirit' or 'ghost.' Many smaller species are indeed nocturnal, with large eyes and a spectral appearance. Like cats, the lemur's eyes have a mirror-like reflecting layer, the tapetum. This helps vision at night and also gives the eerie 'eye-shine' associated with cats' eyes.

There are about 85 species of lemur. Smallest is the pygmy mouse lemur, which at 1oz (30g) is also the smallest primate. Its head and body are hardly larger than a thumb. One of the largest lemurs is the indri or babakoto, with a head-body length of 24in (60cm), a weight of 11-13lb (5-6kg) and an unusually short tail.

The four families of lemur are usually listed as:
- Dwarf and mouse lemurs.
- Typical lemurs, such as the ring-tailed lemur.
- Sportive lemurs.
- Indris, woolly lemurs, sifakas and their cousins.

The smaller lemurs, especially the dwarf and mouse types, are omnivores. They consume a variety of flowers, fruits, buds, leaves, and other plant matter, along with grubs, insects, worms, and similar small creatures. Larger species tend to be more herbivorous, specializing in leaves, flowers, and fruits, and many of these lemurs are diurnal, that is, active during daylight.

Compared to monkeys and chimps, most lemurs have relatively straightforward social lives. Many live in family groups of one female and one male plus their offspring. Only a few, such as the curious aye-aye, are chiefly solitary. Lemurs that form larger social groups tend to be led by one or more older females. This matriarchal society contrasts with the male-led or patriarchal society typical of many monkeys and apes.

Previous pages: The ring-tailed lemur (left) shows the typical lemuroid features of a protruding, almost dog-like muzzle and highly patterned fur. The ruffed lemur's head and neck fur (right) is reminiscent of an old-fashioned ruffed collar.

Above: The sifaka's limbs are long and well-muscled to enable it to perform tremendous springy leaps among the branches. Its powerful fingers and toes grip almost any width of bough.

Opposite: Ring-tailed lemurs are bold, inquisitive, and always alert. Young lemurs start to eat solid food when they are two months old, and are fully weaned at about five months.

The aye-aye

One of the strangest of all primates is the aye-aye, *Daubentonia madagascariensis.* It is slim with coarse fur, mostly dark brown with white or silvery tipped hairs, but paler on the face and underside. It has wide-set, dark-rimmed eyes and gangling limbs. The aye-aye is also the largest nocturnal primate, with a head-body length of 16in (40cm), a bushy tail as long again, and an average weight of 4.4-6.6lb (2-3kg). Its incisors or front gnawing teeth grow continuously, a trait not seen in other primates, but which is typical of rodent mammals, such as rats and mice. Its middle finger on each hand is extraordinarily elongated for probing into tree-trunk holes and under bark for juicy grubs.

In Madagascar, the aye-aye seems to fill the role of a 'nocturnal woodpecker' — these birds are absent from the island. It slinks among the trees in the dark, winkling grubs and insects from under bark. Yet it also consumes fruits and seeds, even gnawing hard nuts, as well as raiding bees' nests for honey.

The aye-aye's suite of strange features, and its unique behavior as the Madagascan version of the woodpecker, make it difficult to classify. It is certainly a primate, but it does not seem to fit in any of the groups. It is usually placed in its own family. Most experts suggest that its closest cousins are the lemurs of the indri family.

Opposite: The indri is well known for its loud, distinctive, song-like calls, which can last from a few seconds to several minutes, but vary in duration and form among different indri groups.

Top: Contrast this typical ruffed lemur's stylish black-and-white coloration with the red variant on page 41. Lemur coloration can be very varied and confusing.

Above: The name sifaka — this is the golden-crowned species — comes from the warning 'sifak' call used on spotting predators.

Left: The aye-aye sniffs out grubs under the bark of trees and uses its slender fingers to winkle its prey from their holes.

Galagos (bushbabies)

The tree-dwelling bushbabies or galagos of Africa are nocturnal, with big eyes and large ears, gray or brown fur, mobile arms, grasping hands, and a long bushy tail. The rear legs are generally long and powerful, for prodigious spring-loaded leaps, often with the body held upright. Some galagos easily leap 10ft (3m) in almost total darkness. Most species prefer forest but some dwell in open woodland and bushy savannah.

The familiar name 'bushbaby' comes from the galago's eerie wails and cries, which echo through the night-time African bush and resemble a human baby or child in distress. Most galagos eat a varied diet of grubs and small animals, fruits, buds, and exudates — sap, gum, resin, and similar juicy fluids that ooze or exude from gnawed trees and bushes. They have keen senses, especially acute night vision conferred by the huge eyes, and large mobile ears that can turn to pinpoint sounds. Using these abilities a galago is able to creep up on small prey, such as a beetle or grub, then with lightning speed suddenly snatch it using its hands. Passing moths are grabbed in mid-air. Small lizards, birds' eggs and chicks, and tree-dwelling mice are also common prey for the larger species.

Most galagos have plain brown-to-gray fur, usually with paler underparts. They sleep by day in a tree hole, leafy nest, or similar secluded site. Some species have quite complex social lives. They share their nests with other females and/or males, according to the season, abundance of food, breeding cycle, and other factors.

There are about 20 species of galagos. Some two-thirds are in the genus, or group of closely related species, known as *Galago*. They include Allen's bushbaby *Galago alleni* and the dusky or Matschie's bushbaby *Galago matschiei*. There are also three species of greater galago in the genus *Otolemur*, including the largest of the galago/bushbaby group. This is the thick-tailed or brown greater bushbaby, which can weigh in excess of 3.3lb (1.5kg). The third genus comprises the needle-clawed galago, *Euoticus*, with a southern and northern species.

Above: It is rare to see a galago out and about in broad daylight. This individual, photographed in Tanzania, Africa, may have been stranded away from its usual nest and is sitting tight, waiting for the cover of dusk before moving.

Opposite: The lesser bushbaby has huge ears, which can swivel independently like radar dishes toward the slightest sounds to detect prey or to help them avoid predators. As well as acute hearing, galagos have large eyes that give them excellent night vision — the time when they are almost exclusively active.

Lorises and pottos

There are two species of slow loris and three of slender loris, all from South and Southeast Asia, and all tropical forest dwellers. Also in the loris family is the potto from tropical Africa, the false potto from West Africa, and two species of angwantibo, also from West Africa, which are sometimes called golden pottos because of their coloration.

All of these primates are mainly secretive tree-dwellers, and little is known about their lifestyles and habits. They range from the size of a domestic cat down to almost as small as a house mouse. They are nocturnal, with brownish fur, a small face, huge eyes, longish body, short tail, and slim limbs of roughly equal length, equipped with hands and feet that can grasp twigs and branches tightly for long periods. The wrist and ankle joints have an exceptionally mobile design, and the thumb can be moved more independently than in other primates (much as in ourselves). With these adaptations, lorises and pottos move slowly and deliberately, rather than leaping at speed like the galagos. They can remain motionless for hours, especially during the day to avoid detection by predators, and when hunting food. Angwantibos and the slender loris tend more to insects, grubs, and other small animal prey, which they capture by stealthy ambush followed by a sudden grab. Slow lorises and pottos eat more fruit and sap or gum, but they still take ants, termites, and similar food items. Almost all of their feeding and resting is done alone, for lorises and pottos are very much solitary creatures. Two of a kind together are usually a male and female at breeding time, or a mother with offspring — in most species there is only one baby per litter.

Opposite: The slow loris curls up in a treetrunk hole or the fork of a branch during the day, to emerge at dusk.

Below: Slow lorises prowl through the foliage at night searching for food — they are carnivores, eating insects and small vertebrates.

Tarsiers

Zoologists have long puzzled as to whether tarsiers are more closely related to monkeys and apes, or to the lemurs, lorises, and bushbabies. Despite their outward appearance, modern studies suggest they belong with the monkeys and apes.

The eight species of tarsier are found only in Southeast Asian forests, from the Philippines to Sumatra, Java, Borneo, and Sulawesi. They are all small, weighing 3.5-5.3oz (100-150g), and when curled up, most could fit into a human hand. Of all primates they have seemingly the hugest eyes, crammed into a small-faced head that is almost as big as the body. Each eyeball is bigger than its owner's brain. The limbs are long and mobile, with elongated ankles and feet adapted for excellent jumps and leaps, while the tail is long but almost hairless.

Tarsiers are tree-dwelling and nocturnal. Western tarsiers tend to be solitary, while other species form small mixed groups, usually based around one male and one female. Tarsiers are also the most carnivorous of all primates. They eat only animal prey, ranging from insects and grubs to small birds, snakes, and lizards.

Opposite and above: The tarsier's eyes are so large in its skull that it cannot swivel them to look around, and so must move its whole head and neck. Tarsiers have strong, sensitive fingers and use them to grip both twigs and prey.

Left: The spectral tarsier has the largest eyes, compared to its body size, of any mammal. This tiny creature is found in Indonesia, particularly in the lowlands of Sulawesi and on Selayar Island.

BEHAVIOR

Lemurs, monkeys, and especially apes are usually regarded as having the most complex and sophisticated behavior of all animals. They have proficient memories, learn from experience, adapt to new conditions and situations, and interact with each other in complicated ways in all their main areas of life — especially feeding, socializing, and breeding. They are the animals we are most likely to call 'clever' and 'intelligent,' because we see in them echoes of many of our own behavioral traits and tendencies.

Food and Feeding

MANY SMALLER species of primates feed largely on insects, grubs, and similar animal-based food items. They might be termed insectivores, although they consume not only insects but also worms, spiders, millipedes, and similar invertebrates. Many other species dine on plant matter, such as saps and fruits, as well as small animal prey, and are more properly termed omnivorous (eating almost anything).

In contrast, most of the larger primate species, including bigger monkeys and almost all of the apes, are mainly vegetarian or herbivorous. They consume a variety of plant matter, from flowers and berries to sap, bark, shoots, nuts, and roots, depending on season and location. But the hallmark of the primate group is adaptability, and when times are hard, many species make do with whatever foods they can obtain.

Unlike most other animals (apart from the occasional squirrel, rat, or raccoon), primates gather in and manipulate their food with their hands. The flexible fingers are well suited to gripping, pulling, and tearing softer food items, and work with the teeth to bite larger pieces into smaller chunks that are easy to swallow. Vision is also very important when foraging amongst vegetation. In particular, monkeys and apes use their acute color vision to discern the changing hues of ripening fruits.

Gums, fruits, and bugs

Among the galagos (bushbabies), which are night-active, there is a wide range of diets. In the Cameroon-Congo region, about three-quarters of the food taken by the Southern needle-clawed bushbaby is plant matter — chiefly gums, saps, and similar juices from trees. This food source is especially rich in sugary nutrients for energy, and is exploited by many smaller primates, including various monkeys. Many of them have a dental arrangement called a 'tooth comb,' in which the long lower front teeth, the incisors, jut forward like the prongs of a rake. The tooth comb is used to run through the fur while grooming, and is also adapted to gouge bark and release gum and sap for licking out with the rough, sandpapery tongue.

The rest of the Southern needle-clawed bushbaby's diet includes insects and similar small animals, even mice and birds, but only occasional fruits. However Allen's bushbaby, found in the same general region of West Africa, eats mostly fruit, with some small animal prey, but little gum or sap. In this way, the two bushbaby species avoid excessive competition for food. Most galagos can snatch prey from leaves, twigs, or the air with their hands, or jerk out their head and neck to snap it up directly into the mouth. Many can even aim at and grab a victim while they themselves are in mid-air during their gravity-defying leaps.

Slowly does it

Among lorises and pottos, about half of the slow loris's diet comprises fruits, and another third is animal prey. The remainder consists of a miscellany of various items, from soft shoots and buds to birds' eggs. The slender loris also eats a mixed selection of insects and other grubs, supplemented by tender leaves, shoots and blossom, and perhaps small lizards, frogs, and rodents.

Most lemurs take a wide-ranging diet, although again there are variations. The dwarf lemurs include more animal prey, from beetles and other insects to lizards such as chameleons, frogs, birds' eggs and chicks. The bamboo lemurs are primate equivalents of the giant panda, living in dense stands of bamboo, which provide more than four-fifths of their diet. The mongoose lemur has a liking for nectar of the kapok tree, and the brown lemur favors spiders, beetles, centipedes, and millipedes.

No plants on the menu

As mentioned earlier, despite their spindly, wide-eyed, innocent appearance, the tarsiers are fierce night-time hunters and the most carnivorous of primates. The Western tarsier has been observed consuming beetles, ants, locusts, crickets, cockroaches, cicadas, caterpillars, moths, praying mantises, spiders, millipedes, small birds such as warblers and pittas plus their eggs and chicks, small frogs, lizards, even poisonous young snakes ...

Previous pages: Orang-utans (left) carefully sniff and taste fruits like this mango for ripeness. A squirrel monkey (right) is attracted by bright-colored ripe berries.

Above: Despite its name, the slow loris moves surprisingly quickly to grab a crunchy beetle.

Opposite: A ring-tailed lemur demonstrates the characteristic primate trait of hand-manipulating food.

Monkey food

The feeding habits of most monkeys can be described as 'opportunistic.' Many of them mix and match plant and animal matter, adapting to the season and local availability. Because most species are group-dwelling, food gathering is often a social affair. As individuals forage, they dart watchful glances at fellow troop members. If one finds a rich food source, the others soon crowd around and try to join in. Their success depends largely on their position in the troop hierarchy. A senior member can repel junior colleagues, but a lowly ranked individual may find its food source quickly commandeered by those of higher status.

In some marmosets over half of the food intake is gums, saps, and other exudates; for the pygmy marmoset this proportion rises to two-thirds. Tamarins focus more on fruits, complemented by small animal prey. Up to half of the red howler monkey's dietary intake is young leaves, from more than 150 different plant species. Indeed the fruit- and seed-eating monkeys, apes, and other primates play valuable roles in maintaining the ecology of their forests. The resistant seeds pass through their guts and emerge in the droppings, to fall onto the ground where they germinate, thereby aiding dispersal of plant species.

Predatory instincts

Some monkeys have a taste for larger meaty items. In the New World, white-throated capuchins occasionally munch baby squirrels, and brown-fronted capuchins chew bats. In Southeast Asia the crab-eating macaque does certainly eat crabs, but more than half its diet is plant material, especially fruits; these monkeys can be serious pests as they raid farm crops.

Baboons are large, powerful Old World monkeys and some catch substantial animal prey, up to the size of hares, young bushpigs, and even small gazelles. In Southern Africa, Chacma baboons living along the coast feast on shellfish, such as mussels and limpets, crabs, and other seafoods. The colobus or leaf monkeys have a specialized stomach with pouches containing plentiful 'friendly' bacteria that help to break down their otherwise fairly indigestible leafy food.

Below left: Marmosets feed mainly after dawn and before dusk, on a diet of insects, spiders, small vertebrates, birds' eggs, and tree sap.

Below: Crab-eating macaques forage among mangrove roots at low tide for crabs, shrimps, and other shellfish.

Opposite: Blue monkeys spend time chewing their leafy food to help release its limited nutrients.

Fussy eaters

Larger monkeys with restricted diets include the rare gelada baboon of Ethiopia's high grasslands. More than 90 percent of its food is grass, picked by nimble fingers as the baboon bottom-shuffles along. The proboscis monkey of Southeast Asia frequents coastal mangrove swamps and eats large quantities of their leaves, as well as seeds and fruits — mostly unripe. This material is low in nutrients, and so is needed in copious quantities. After a large meal, around half the total weight of a proboscis monkey may be its stomach contents.

Ape feasts

Among the apes, most of the gibbons have a diet of one-half to two-thirds fruit, along with leaves and shoots, and some animal prey. An exception is the black gibbon, which eats mainly leaves and shoots of more than 50 plant species, including bamboo.

Orang-utans prefer large, succulent fruits — especially durian, which to most humans smells repugnant. Like other monkeys and apes, oranges use various clues to find their food. These include smell, especially to locate blossom and the powerful odors of ripening fruits, also the sight of colorful fruits in their ripe condition, the movements of other creatures such as monkeys and birds toward a rich food source, and the feeding noises of these consumers as they squabble at a site.

Lowland gorillas are also keen fruit-eaters, along with leaves, pith, and soft bark, plus a snack of termites almost daily. Mountain gorillas tend more to leaves, buds, shoots, and stems, with only a small proportion of fruits and animal prey. Gorilla eating is a leisurely affair, with up to 14 hours spent foraging and interacting socially. Like many day-active primates, gorillas feed mainly during the first three to four hours of daylight, with a smaller peak of activity toward dusk.

Above: Young orang-utans spend years observing their mothers feeding. Gradually they learn to recognize the sights and smells of the best fruits, and recall the localities of fruiting trees in the dense forests where they live.

Opposite: Gorillas are surrounded by their food and spend much time sniffing and touching possible items, to select only the most tasty and juiciest morsels to eat.

Smart dining

Common chimpanzees are chiefly herbivores, with leaves, fruits, flowers, and seeds forming 90 percent of the diet. However chimps are famed for their wide-ranging tastes, and for the tools used to obtain food. They 'fish' for termites or ants using a long, slim item — a ready-made twig or stem, or one modified by stripping its leaves. The 'rod' is poked into a nest opening causing the insects to swarm over it, then the chimp withdraws it and quickly licks them off. Alternatively a chimp may break open the nest with a bigger puncturing stick. Palm oil nuts and similar hard-cased items are cracked open using a pebble as a hammer and a flat stone or tree root as an anvil.

In a relatively new study, chimpanzees have been observed using sticks to jab or spear small animals hiding in tree holes, such as bushbabies and squirrels. Marauding gangs of chimps also pursue animals on noisy hunts. This behavior has a strong social content, as is explained later.

Above: When selecting a stone as a hammer to crack nuts, the chimp tests several for the correct weight and balance. Anvil sites, usually hard roots or flat rocks, are valuable places and chimps may queue to use them. Recent research indicates that chimpanzees have used stone tools for at least 4500 years.

Above: A chimp may bite and fray the end of a termite-fishing stick.

Opposite: The chimpanzee's diet is omnivorous, but mainly vegetarian, consisting of leaves, fruits, nuts, seeds, tubers, and other vegetation, supplemented by insects and small vertebrates.

Social Life

LEMURS, MONKEYS, and apes who live in groups show a whole range of types of society and social interactions. Group size ranges from a handful to more than 200 in certain monkey troops, such as capuchins. In some species females take the lead, while in others males are in charge. There is usually a hierarchy or pecking order, as some individuals become dominant and have first choice of food, shelter and mates, while submissive ones wait for leaner pickings. Selected troop members form profitable 'best-friend' alliances while others always seem to be in dispute with each other.

All of these interactions change through time as new troop members are born or arrive from outside, while others die or are cast out. As with many aspects of monkey and ape behavior, we can appreciate these social characterisitics by extension from our own human experiences with family and friends.

Communication

Monkeys and apes socialize using a wide range of communication methods. There are visual signs, such as facial expressions and body postures, dozens of sounds from alarm shrieks to reassuring murmurs, and a variety of scents from bodily gland secretions. These send out information about current conditions and future intentions, such as hunger, friendliness, aggression, fear, and warning. However, we must avoid projecting too much of our human experience onto them. For example, a chimp may seem to us to be grinning broadly. In fact it is probably showing apprehension, or even fear, by pulling back its lips to reveal its large teeth, which it will not hesitate to use in self defense.

Physical contact is also very important for primates, who use pats, cuddles, cuffs, smacks, and slaps in much the same way as humans do. In particular, most monkey and ape species employ mutual grooming as a social tool. Individuals run their fingers or teeth through the fur of others, not only to remove tangles, dirt, and pests, such as fleas and lice, but also to strengthen bonds of friendship or show which animal is dominant.

Females on top

Ring-tailed lemurs live in relatively stable, mixed, female-dominated groups of up to 20 individuals, perhaps more if food is plentiful. Within the group the females and males have separate hierarchies, with a spectrum ranging from the most dominant to most submissive individuals. Rank is established by baring teeth, lunging, cuffing, scratching, biting and similar actions, and also smearing smelly glandular secretions onto the long furry tail and waving it in the face of rivals. Females always win these battles against males.

Among the female ring-tails, one core female line is usually dominant, with an older mother who is the overall boss, and a variety of sisters and daughters. They stay close, interact plentifully and mutually groom. There may be another one or two female lines in the troop, but relationships between the lines are less friendly. Females usually stay in the troop where they were born, while males come in from other groups. There are usually two or three dominant males per troop who gain the most mating favors. Other males are peripheral — not only in social interactions, but they also stay around the edges of the troop as it travels, feeds, and rests.

Alpha males

Among New World monkeys, there is a whole spectrum of social systems, even among closely related species. Monk and white-faced sakis tend to live in family groups of a breeding pair plus offspring, while bearded sakis form larger multi-male, multi-female troops. Brown capuchins roam in mixed troops with roughly equal numbers of males and females, although one individual, the alpha male, is dominant.

Previous pages: Japanese macaques (left) bathe socially in a hot spring during winter, with 'friends' staying close together. In the Himalayas of Nepal, the morning sunbathe is a time for macaques (right) to renew social contacts.

He takes the lead when searching for food and shelter, and when disputing territory with neighboring troops. He also defends his troop and especially his own offspring, not only against incoming capuchin males from other troops, but even against predators. If birds of prey appear, he makes loud, sharp alarm whistles to draw attention to himself and warn the others to flee.

Right: *The brown capuchin alpha male is often occupied keeping other males in the troop in their place, and resisting incomers from other groups who aim to usurp his power.*

Below: *The blood lines of female ring-tailed lemurs dominate their society. Males are socially subordinate in all respects, even in feeding, allowing the females to eat first. Males are marginalized from group activity, and alternate between troops every three to four years.*

Gorilla family life

Although the typical gorilla group is dominated by a large mature male, the silverback, in about one-third of mountain gorilla groups there may be two such males, who form a truce while food and other resources are plentiful. About half of females leave their troop of birth at around the age of eight years, and most males have gone by the age of eleven. These males live alone or with other young bachelors until they reach sufficient size and power to attract their own females, or more rarely, challenge the silverback of an existing group for its leadership.

Within a gorilla troop, there is little sign of any dominance hierarchy among females. Much of the quiet midday period is spent in relaxation, mutual grooming, and indulging youngsters in play, with relaxed relationships between all troop members.

Above: *The mature male or silverback gorilla watches over his females and will charge toward any danger, whether from unfamiliar males looking for a mate to add to their harem or predatory big cats, such as leopards, which have strayed too close.*

Left: *As young gorillas socialize, they learn to recognize the subtle body postures and behavioral patterns that signal dominance or submission within the group.*

Chimp clubs

Common chimpanzees, like gorillas, inhabit male-dominated societies, with community size ranging from less than 20 to more than 100. However, it is not one male but a small group of related males, such as fathers, sons, and brothers — a 'brotherhood' — who take charge. They are together for much of the time, patrol the territorial boundaries, and instigate hunting parties or attacks on neighboring troops. In these aggressive pursuits, males coordinate to drive the victim into an ambush, and then tear it to pieces and consume it, with other favored troop members sharing the bloody meal. Since animal meat forms only a small part of a chimp's diet, the significance of these hunts may lie more in reinforcing the bonds and dominance of the brotherhood, and in gifting 'favors' to lesser members (such as females around mating time), than in nutrition.

Within the overall chimp community, subordinate males, females, and their offspring associate more loosely. Two or three females may form a short-term coalition, but these relationships are very fluid and changeable. Individuals and small parties frequently join and subsequently leave, in a social system known as 'fission-fusion.'

Chimps communicate by means of dozens of facial gestures and grimaces, body postures and actions, and more than 40 well-known sounds and calls, ranging from whimpers to screams. A common sound is the pant-hoot, a rising 'woo-hoo-hoo' for various social situations.

Sex and society

Bonobos (pygmy chimps) are generally less frantic than their common cousins. They form large communities of up to 200 that split into subgroups of five to 15 when feeding. Most grooming and similar interactions are female-female, with fewest being male-male. Aggressive encounters are generally scarce, and even neighboring communities tend to avoid each other rather than confront one another.

A striking feature of bonobos is their frequent, open use of sexual acts, from gentle genital rubbing to full intercourse, in many social situations. Young and old partake, and the events may be mixed- or same-sex. Often these acts are a way of defusing tension after an antagonistic encounter, such as squabbling over a piece of food. But even casual meetings may involve sex as a 'Hello!' Or sex can be a way of reinforcing a close friendship, beginning an alliance, or a bribe to share food.

Above: Bonobos indulge in plenty of close physical contact, including simulated and actual sex on a casual basis.

Opposite: A chimp's grimace highlights its teeth as a warning that it is ready to use them, not only on enemies but on rivals for status within the community.

Courtship and Breeding

APES, MONKEYS, and other primates participate in a wide spectrum of breeding behaviors. There are mother-only one-parent families in orang-utans, to extended families, with one main breeding pair and others helping with babycare, in many smaller South American monkeys.

The primate group as a whole shows three distinctive trends in reproduction. First, pregnancy (gestation) is relatively long compared to most mammals of similar size. In a rhesus macaque it is 160-165 days; in a brown hare by comparison, 42 days. Second, primate mothers usually bear just one, or less often two, young, rather than the large litters seen in mammals such as rodents. Third, parental care is thorough and extended. Larger apes nurture their offspring for longer than almost any other mammals apart from elephants.

Smelly contests

In the female-dominated society of ring-tailed lemurs, breeding is polygynous, that is, one male mates with several females. In spring the females howl, scratch, and fight for access to a male. All the females in a troop come into breeding condition within 10-14 days, so this time sees frenzied sexual activity. The babies are born some four months later in August. The mother feeds, grooms, and cares for her young, who clings to her belly and then rides on her back, and becomes independent after about five months.

Most lorises, bushbabies, and tarsiers are generally solitary, and pair up only at mating time. Courtship is brief and unspectacular, lasting perhaps only minutes, then the male plays no further part. The mother carries and cares for her young, usually one but perhaps two. She may 'park' them in a nest as she goes off to feed. Sometimes two or three females with young share a sleeping nest.

Families and harems

Among New World monkeys, the golden lion tamarins of southeast Brazil form smallish family groups of up to eight closely related members. The senior male

and female are the breeding pair. Their older offspring stay on for a time to help rear the newest one or two babies. At first the young cling to their mother, but from about the fourth week they venture away to explore and play. Unusually for primates, at this time the father may take the lead in child care.

At the other end of the monkey spectrum, in West Africa the large and powerful mandrill male chases away rival males and dominates his harem of several females, enjoying exclusive mating rights. Females breed at between four and eight years of age, giving birth to one young every two years. Other females in the group — sisters, aunts, nieces — help with baby care.

Importance of territory

Most gibbons form long-term pairs with very strong female-male bonds. They also actively pronounce occupancy of their territory by calling loudly, because a gibbon without a territory is unlikely to breed. One baby is the norm, every two to four years. By the age of ten years, offspring leave the parental family, team up with a partner and try to carve out their own territory, or occupy one when the residents die.

Territories are also important to the orang-utan. The fully mature male occupies a very large range, which contains the smaller overlapping areas of several females. Males are very forceful in mating, despite the females' often vigorous protests. Less mature males, who are nonetheless sexually active, may sneak in and copulate with a female while the resident older male's attentions are elsewhere in his range.

An orang baby is cared for and nurtured for longer than any other primate. It watches and imitates its mother carefully as she selects and tries food items, and learns foraging techniques and the fruiting patterns of different trees through the seasons. Youngsters stay with their mothers for between five and seven years, so the interval between successive births may be eight or more years. This slow reproductive rate has grave consequences for the survival of the two orang species, as described later.

Previous pages: A baby orang-utan (left) clings tightly to its mother's fur. Young baboons (right) stay close to, and copy, their mothers' actions.

Above: Gibbons call loudly at dawn and dusk to maintain dominance in their all-important territory.

Opposite: A male mandrill will not hesitate to threaten rivals with his dagger-like canine teeth.

Gorilla babies

Gorillas, by and large, pursue a sedate sex life. The few females in a troop mate only with their silverback, after a brief courtship where he struts, chest-beats, and sniffs her sexual organs, while she crouches and backs toward him, perhaps leaping onto his back as the couple 'coo.' After a pregnancy of about eight and a half months (just less than the human's nine months) the baby is born helpless and almost devoid of fur. By seven weeks it can reach out to grip, with crawling being achieved by nine weeks, first solid foods at 12 weeks, riding on the mother's back at four months, walking and climbing by six months, and weaning at three years. As with chimps, young gorillas play with other troop youngsters, parents, and carers. They jump about, roll, wrestle and play tag and king-of-the-castle, as they develop their strength and coordination, all the time watched over by the parents.

Chimp culture

Common chimpanzees have a promiscuous lifestyle and courtship is unsophisticated. Baby chimps are born with pink faces, which gradually darken with age. They follow a similar development pattern to young gorillas, although they take to the trees and climb more readily. From the age of about four months the young chimp watches its mother and other adults closely as they forage. Gradually it learns tool tricks such as termite fishing and nut cracking, thereby passing on knowledge from one generation to the next, which leads us to refer to 'culture' when discussing these great apes.

Right: Like human babies, ape youngsters need plenty of rest. As the group moves to a new feeding area, very young offspring are cradled in their mothers' arms. After a few months their muscles and sense of balance are developed enough to ride on her back.

CONSERVATION

Monkeys, apes, and their cousins evolved in trees, and more than 90 percent of their species still live in tropical and subtropical forests. But in today's world, timber, and then the cleared land where trees once grew, are valuable commodities. More than 100 primate species are considered threatened from habitat loss and various other dangers, from poaching to the effects of pollution and warfare. Some are being saved by strenuous conservation efforts, but too many others are almost unnoticed, on the brink of extinction.

Threats and Dangers

BY FAR the greatest threat facing the natural world is habitat loss. This overarching term encompasses the disappearance of unspoilt wild places due to varied human activities, from the building of new towns, roads, factories, and leisure facilities, to habitats degraded by pollution, mining, and other industries, or cleared for farm crops and livestock. In warmer, well-forested parts of the world, the monkeys, apes, lemurs, and other primates are in the thick of the struggle. Like the millions of creatures and plants they live with, making up intricate and delicate webs of nature, many species are losing out.

Orang-utans in peril

Habitat loss is vividly illustrated by the desperate plight of the two orang-utan species. On the 'Red Lists' of threatened creatures and plants drawn up by the IUCN (International Union for the Conservation of Nature and Natural Resources), the Bornean orang is in the 'Endangered' category, and the situation of the Sumatran orang is even more grave at 'Critically Endangered.' In their cases, habitat loss is chiefly due to logging of the tropical forests for hardwood timber, or simply burning down the trees — not only illegally, in the face of weak law enforcement, but also legally, due to corrupt agreements. After forest clearances come crops, especially oil palm plantations. These yield the world's most widely produced vegetable oil with myriad uses in cooking, processed foods, industry, and as biofuels. Palm oil products are sold around the world. So we, as consumers, are indirectly fueling the orang-utan's problems.

Bushmeat and pets

Dwindling habitats mean the Bornean orang population has shrunk to less than 40,000, while the Sumatran species probably numbers less than 5000. Apart from habitat loss, threats include the bushmeat and pet trades. Bushmeat is a fast-growing problem for many primates, especially monkeys and apes in West Africa, more recently in Asia, and for monkeys in South America. The animals are hunted and butchered, and the meat is eaten by the hunters or sold at market — often openly, despite wildlife conservation laws. Baby orangs and other primates are also captured alive as 'exotic pets'. This usually necessitates killing the mother, who tries desperately to protect her offspring.

Dire predictions include the loss of the Sumatran orang by 2025 unless there are massive conservation efforts. Orang-utans have a high public profile, but of course the loss of Southeast Asian forests also threatens many other primates, including various species of gibbon, langur monkey, and tarsier.

Previous pages: As new ports and coastal leisure facilities develop in Southeast Asia, the proboscis monkey's (left) mangrove habitat shrinks. Fragmented habitats mean that a male orang-utan (right) may not achieve a full breeding range.

Above: Orang-utan babies are stolen from their mothers and passed through the international smuggling system to become prized 'pets' in a private collection.

Gorilla trouble

The Western gorilla has recently been shifted from IUCN's 'Endangered' to 'Critically Endangered' category. Its numbers have more than halved in the past 25 years. Apart from logging and habitat clearance, the bushmeat trade in all kinds of West African wildlife has burgeoned to a commercial scale. Also the deadly Ebola virus, which affects humans, has killed more than half of the gorillas in some areas.

Mountain gorillas are also victims of human-borne diseases, as well as forest clearance, occasional bushmeat kills, and even 'commissions' for capture of live young by unscrupulous wildlife dealers. With only 600–700 individuals left, these rarest of gorillas are teetering on the edge of extinction.

Widespread risks

For every high-profile threatened ape or monkey, such as the orang-utan or gorilla, there are numerous less well-known primate species facing severe dangers. Madagascar is a global 'hot spot' for biodiversity (range of animals and plants). Much of its wildlife, especially its lemurs, is unique. But the island is experiencing immense pressures from its people for living space, farming, and industry, which is eating away at its fragile natural habitats.

Four of the 25 most threatened primates, as listed by the IUCN's Primate Specialist Group, are from Madagascar. They are the greater bamboo lemur, white-collared lemur, silky sifaka, and Sahamalaza sportive lemur. The silky sifaka of northeastern Madagascar is the 'flagship' species of a recently proposed World Heritage Site, Marojejy National Park. Even so, local people hunt these lemurs for food or because they eat the leaves of crops, which is known as 'revenge killing'. Trees in the habitat are felled for firewood, charcoal, and valuable timbers like rosewood.

Opposite: Javan or ebony langurs are trapped as pets or for food, despite legal protection as an officially 'endangered' species.

At risk in the New World

The IUCN list of 25 most threatened primates includes three New World monkeys: the brown spider monkey, brown-headed spider monkey, and yellow-tailed woolly monkey. This last species was thought to be extinct from the 1920s. It was rediscovered in 1974 in the tropical Andes foothills of eastern Peru, in cloud forests at altitudes of about 5000 to 8200ft (1500 to 2500m). But parts of its home range are being replaced by towns, roads, and farming, as a result of the unrestrained development blighting the Amazon region. This leads to a serious problem associated with habitat loss — habitat fragmentation.

Habitat fragmentation occurs when a species' natural range is gradually split into smaller isolated 'islands' by encroaching areas of human activity and development. The species' members can no longer find enough food or establish the territories and home ranges they need for breeding. Fragmentation also limits dispersal of individuals to new areas. Normally this dispersal avoids the problems of inbreeding and 'genetic staleness' in the breeding population. As a result habitat fragmentation can mean that, even if the overall population numbers of a species look hopeful, only small, separate, genetically cut-off groups survive, which are not viable in the long term.

The yellow-tailed woolly monkey suffers further because its long, thick fur, especially the yellow tufts on the underside of the tail, are prized as trophies or souvenirs. This fate of ending up as hunting trophies affects many other monkey and ape species. Another New World primate on the 'Critically Endangered' list is the northern muriqui (woolly spider monkey), with just a few hundred left in the world.

Opposite: Red uakaris are suffering from a shrinking, fragmented distribution in Brazil, Colombia, and Peru.

Above right: Woolly spider monkeys are among the rarest monkeys.

Right: Fewer than 250 brown spider monkeys survive in the wild.

Reserves and Sanctuaries

SINCE HABITAT loss is by far the major threat facing much of the world's wildlife, including apes, monkeys, and their primate cousins, the remedy would seem obvious: stop habitat loss. In fact, reverse it and achieve habitat restoration. For example, devastated tropical forests might be rescued, replanted, and protected as they grow again and their monkeys, apes, and other wildlife return.

Of course, the modern world does not work like this. In tropical forest regions, many people barely manage to eke out an impoverished existence. To achieve the lifestyles enjoyed by rich industrialized nations, they develop their industries and agriculture. Saving threatened primates and other wildlife is low on the list of priorities.

Yet rare animal species — especially gorillas, chimps, orang-utans, monkeys, and lemurs — are themselves a valuable resource. People pay to come and see them, bringing eco-tourist money to the region, which can then be used for sustainable development that respects local natural heritage. One of the main ways of utilizing this wildlife resource is to set aside areas as reserves, parks, and sanctuaries, where animals, plants, and all of nature are protected from interference, damage, and development.

Gorilla mountains

Mountain gorillas are among the most restricted and endangered of all animals. Their predicament is recognized by the three Central African countries where they live — DR Congo, Uganda, and Rwanda. The main mountain gorilla homeland, with about 350 individuals, is the Virunga Range of extinct volcanoes along the junction of their national borders. Three parks are designated for their protection: DR Congo's Virunga National Park, Rwanda's Volcans National Park, and Uganda's Mgahinga National Park. A separate population of 290 mountain gorillas lives in the Bwindi Impenetrable National Park, Uganda. The World Heritage Site of Bwindi is especially fascinating since it also harbors common chimpanzees, as well as monkeys including vervets, baboons, colobus, and several guenon species. As home of the Bwindi Impenetrable Great Ape Project, many scientists carry out research work here, especially on the relationships between the mountain gorillas and chimps, two apes who occur together nowhere else.

Mountain gorillas are some of the most highly monitored and protected creatures in the world, under the eye of ranger patrols and guard centers. Yet still losses occur, including poaching for bushmeat and gorillas trapped by snares set for other forest animals. The terrain is dense and difficult, and it's impossible to observe all comings and goings. An added difficulty is tribal conflict in the region, which makes eco-tourism and even ranger patrolling so dangerous.

Waging war

Salonga National Park (which is the size of the Netherlands) in DR Congo was created in 1970 specifically to safeguard the bonobo (pygmy chimp), in the only country where it lives. But the region is plagued by civil unrest, conflict, and open warfare. Policing the park properly is not possible under such conditions. Hunting is illegal, but armed gangs often enter the park. They are part of the commercial bushmeat trade, or members of armed militias hiding out in the thick forest, where they subsist by killing local animals — including bonobos.

Because of the dense forest conditions, estimates of bonobo populations vary enormously from 10,000 to 50,000. Most observers agree that the population has crashed in the past 30 years. The 2000s saw renewed hope with the creation of several new bonobo sanctuary areas including Lomako-Yokokala, Tumba-Ledima, and Sankuru (which is the size of Belgium) all in DR Congo.

Orang-utan hopes

Perhaps the most famous orang site is Sepilok Orang-Utan Rehabilitation Center in the Kabili-Sepilok Forest Reserve of Sabah, northern Borneo. Here orphaned young orangs, and those rescued from being pets, are gradually introduced to the ways of the wild by trained keepers. In the wild, a young orang-utan learns an enormous amount, especially what to eat, by watching its mother. Sepilok's carers act as surrogates to help the orangs learn the skills they need for independent survival, as well as raising money and public awareness with more than 70,000 visitors each year.

Previous pages: Close-up views and personal encounters with gorillas (left and right) are only possible after many patient months of habituation — getting them used to non-threatening human presence.

Above: Salonga National Park is Africa's largest tropical rainforest reserve, a UNESCO World Heritage Site in Danger, and the main hope for the highly threatened bonobo.

Opposite: At Borneo's Sepilok Center, young orang-utans are tutored in the ways of the wild — but 'the wild' is fast disappearing.

Lion of Brazil

An encouraging monkey conservation effort focuses on the golden lion tamarin of Brazil. For years its specialized habitat of Atlantic coastal rainforest was logged and cleared for agriculture, until only 2 percent of the original area remained. The tamarins were captured in large numbers for zoos, the pet trade and laboratory testing. By the 1960s this squirrel-sized species' population was fewer than 200.

Massive publicity brought a public groundswell, no doubt helped by the tamarin's cute, cuddly looks. It became a 'flagship' species, symbolic of the risks facing Brazilian wildlife. Government, industry, and local sponsors rallied to the effort. Captive breeding programs were established in zoos around the world. In 1974 the Poco das Antas Biological Reserve was created in Rio de Janeiro State, supplemented by privately owned lands to provide a protected area of 41,000 acres (16,600 hectares). Reintroductions of captive-bred tamarins to the wild commenced in 1984. By the mid 2000s the total wild population (not counting captive breeding colonies) was rising toward 1400, and the species' Red List status was amended from 'Critically Endangered' to 'Endangered.'

Helpful measures

Captive breeding is important for several primate species, from lemurs to gorillas. As with racehorses, zoos and wildlife parks maintain 'stud books' that track the genetic history of individuals and groups, so they can bring together suitable partners for mating, without the risks of inbreeding.

CITES, the Convention on International Trade in Endangered Species, prevents selling or trade in animal parts and products such as skins, fur, and internal organs that are sometimes used in traditional medicines. All primates are included in Appendix II of the convention, meaning trade is licensed on a permit-only basis. More than 60 species, from the aye-aye to the Zanzibar colobus, including all apes, are given Appendix I total protection.

Above: More than 100 zoos worldwide support over 550 captive golden lion tamarins, breeding them for reintroduction into the wild. Individual tamarins are regularly swapped to counter any tendency to inbreeding.

Opposite: The Zanzibar (Kirk's) red colobus has been adopted as the flagship species for wildlife conservation programs in the island archipelago of Zanzibar, off the coast of the Tanzanian mainland, East Africa.

The Future

APES, MONKEYS, and other primates are increasingly part of our lives in so many ways. Scientists continue to make amazing discoveries about primates. Their findings range from how diseases are transmitted to the nature of intelligence and development of culture. Medical experiments on primates are controversial, with supporters saying that no other 'animal model' predicts so closely how life-saving treatments will affect humans. Such experiments have led to new vaccines and therapies for asthma and kidney failure. Although most primates used in laboratory research in the US are domestically-bred around 14,000 monkeys are imported annually.

Apes, monkeys, and lemurs have important roles to play in the future of nature conservation. We identify with their intricate behavior, intelligence, and complex social lives. Gorillas, chimps, orang-utans, woolly monkeys, baboons, lemurs, and other high-profile species act as 'flagship' awareness-raisers for wildlife campaigns. They become the focus for conservation efforts such as setting up reserves, parks, and sanctuaries, which benefit all the creatures and plants of the area. But respecting these protected areas depends on tackling complex human issues, such as poverty, corruption, and conflict, so that local people reap some benefit.

More than 30 kinds of primates, from the Cross River gorilla and Sumatran orang-utan to the brown spider monkey, Sri Lankan slender loris, and Sia Island tarsier, are at risk of disappearing from our planet within the next 20-30 years. Only vigorous, well-funded, sustainable, and international conservation efforts can save them, and ensure the future of some of the most complex, fascinating, and entrancing creatures in the world.

Opposite: In Southern Africa, troops of Chacma baboons have become a menace as they overturn rubbish bins and even enter houses in their search for food.

Above: The endangered slender loris is widely trapped and killed for use in folk remedies and also for use as a laboratory animal.

Fascinating Facts

Size

- The biggest ape, and largest primate, is the mature male gorilla (silverback), which weighs more than 441lb (200kg).
- The smallest apes are gibbon species such as Kloss's gibbon and the white-handed gibbon, at around 11lb (5kg).
- The biggest monkey is the mandrill, weighing more than 66lb (30kg).
- The smallest monkey is the pygmy marmoset, weighing up to 3.5oz (100g).
- The largest lemurs are the indri and diademed sifaka, at around 15lb (7kg).
- The smallest lemur, and most diminutive primate, is the pygmy mouse lemur, at 1oz (30g).

Body proportions

The intermembral index, IM, is the ratio of arm length to leg length. The higher it is, the longer are the arms in relation to the whole body.

Guereza (Eastern black-and-white colobus) 78

Human 80

Olive baboon 95

Chimp 100

Black spider monkey 105

Gorilla 115

Siamang (largest gibbon) 140

Lifestyle and habits

- An adult male gorilla may eat more than 44lb (20kg) of (mostly plant) food daily, compared to a human's intake of 3.3lb (1.5kg).
- The only solely nocturnal monkeys are the douroucoulis, also called night or owl monkeys, of South America. They have huge eyes and make owl-like hoots.
- Douroucoulis are also the most caring primate fathers. Apart from when the mother suckles, the male carries the offspring for the first two months.
- Gibbons are usually regarded as the fastest primates, when they move by arm-swinging or brachiation. Speeds reach 39ft per second (12m/sec), with single swings of 50ft (15m), compared to the gibbon's maximum walking speed of 10ft per second (3m/sec).
- The slender loris washes its hands, feet, and face in its own urine, to scent-mark its territory and perhaps also to soothe insect bites.
- The oldest recorded age for a primate is that of the chimpanzee Cheeta (private name Jiggs). Co-star of several *Tarzan* films in the 1930s-40s, he was 75 years old in April 2007.

Above: *The indri is Madagascar's largest wild primate.*

Above: The tailless Barbary macaque is found in the Atlas Mountains of Algeria and Morocco with a small, possibly introduced, population living wild in Gibraltar.

Distribution

- The Cross River gorilla (a subspecies of the Western lowland gorilla) is found in fragmented areas totaling only 77sq miles (200km²) near the Cameroon-Nigeria border.
- After the human, the primate with the widest distribution is the rhesus macaque, which ranges from Afghanistan to China.
- Japanese macaques or 'snow monkeys' live farther north than any other primate. They cope with winter temperatures of 5°F (−15°C) by resting in natural volcanic hot springs where the water can be more than 104°F (40°C).
- Only one primate species lives wild in Europe. This is the Barbary macaque, also known as the 'Barbary ape,' although it is a monkey, not an ape. A small colony of about 200–250 individuals lives in the Gibraltar area at the southern tip of Spain, including on the rock itself.

Monkeys and people

- The rhesus blood groups Rh+ and Rh− in humans were named for the discovery of similar blood groups in rhesus macaque monkeys.
- Hanuman langurs are named for the Hindu monkey god Hanuman and are sacred to many people, being fed with handouts of blessed food, especially at temples.
- Several kinds of monkeys, from capuchins to macaques, are trained to harvest fruits, such as ripe coconuts, at plantations.
- Uakari monkeys are said to be named from a local South American word for Europeans, since their bald, reddish faces reminded the local people of sunburned white Europeans.
- Among the cleverest monkeys are capuchins, especially the brown or tufted capuchins. They have been trained as companions to do tasks for paralyzed people, and even as 'reconnaissance officers' for the US police, equipped with video camera, two-way radio, and mini bullet-proof vest.

Above: Hanuman langurs are a familiar sight to Indian city dwellers.

Index